NETWORKING FOR A/E/C PROFESSIONALS
A Blueprint for Seller-Doers

150+ TIPS TO BECOME A BETTER NETWORKER!

Scott D. Butcher, FSMPS, CPSM

© 2018 by Scott D. Butcher.

Cover photo and chapter divider photos licensed from Adobe Stock.

Contact information:

    Scott D. Butcher, FSMPS, CPSM
    Vice President & CMO
    JDB Engineering, Inc.
    3687 Concord Road
    York, PA 17402
    717.434.1543
    sbutcher@jdbe.com

    www.jdbengineering.com

jdbIQity helps your business plan for tomorrow by providing meaningful intelligence, marketing strategy, business development prowess, training, and facilitation. Whether acting as your Outsourced CMO or helping to cultivate your staff's skills, our team is focused on helping you elevate your Business IQ through our three pillars of Imagine, Innovate, Impact. Our team members are current practitioners, living "in the trenches" daily and bringing unique, current insight to our clients. Interested to learn more about how jdbIQity can help position your practice to meet the challenges ahead? We'd love to chat! Visit www.jdbe.com/jdbiqity.

JDB Engineering is not your typical engineering firm. We're committed to transformation, whether helping our clients transform their facilities or helping to transform our industry. A fully-integrated engineering firm focused on buildings and systems, JDB Engineering believes strongly that the best engineering solutions are born through creativity in problem-solving. We draw inspiration from blue skies and blue oceans – that is, innovation and new ways of looking at things. With a corporate focus on **Engineering with Creativity ... Leadership by Design**, we're ready to successfully transform your next project! Learn more at www.jdbengineering.com.

Ready to learn more? Contact Scott D. Butcher, FSMPS, CPSM at sbutcher@jdbe.com or 717.434.1543.

Introduction & Acknowledgements

So why another book about networking? Aren't there already enough out there? Sure, there are dozens – perhaps *hundreds* – of books about how to build networks and how to become a better networker. I own many of them! And yet, there seemed to be two holes within the realm of networking books:

1. Books specific to the architectural, engineering, and construction (A/E/C) industry
2. A quick-reference "how-to" guide for professionals thrust into networking situations

Thus *Networking for A/E/C Professionals: A Blueprint for Seller-Doers*. This isn't so much a book as it is a presentation! In fact, the genesis of this guide is a lunch-and-learn presentation I gave to my coworkers.

As part of my firm's Business Development University, I invited a friend to give a presentation to my coworkers, which became a quid pro quo! This friend, William R. Long, PE, LEED AP, FSMPS, associate vice president of P. Agnes in Philadelphia, came to JDB Engineering's office to present "Network is a Collective Noun; Networking is an Action Verb." Afterward, a coworker and I traveled to Bill's office to present about Building Information Modeling. In both cases, it was network-building. Bill's networking presentation focused on where to find and how to build your networks, with tips about what to do at a networking function.

His presentation was well-received; however, as he was pulling out of our parking lot, a younger staff member stopped in my office and said, "That was really helpful – but I still don't feel comfortable when I'm at a networking event. How do I start a conversation with a stranger? What am I supposed to do while I'm there?" Those questions led me to create a sequel to Bill's presentation: "Casting the Net: Networks and Networking 2.0." I presented it originally for staff, then was invited to give it to several engineering groups. It is now part of JDB Engineering's AIA CES program, and we offer 1.0 AIA LU each time I give it! (www.jdbengineering.com/AIA)

Although I almost never present with notes, I am fairly diligent about compiling notes within my PowerPoint slide deck, which helps me formulate what I'm going to say as I build the presentation, and reminds me of what I originally wanted to say every time I subsequently give the program. My somewhat detailed notes created the foundation for this book, which is why you'll find it so conversational in tone.

So reference this before you go to your next networking event, and keep it handy to use as a refresher in the future!

TABLE OF CONTENTS

One	Why Networking is Important
Two	What Networking Is & Isn't
Three	Who Belongs in Your Network?
Four	Before the Event
Five	Know Thyself
Six	During the Event
Seven	How to Determine if Someone Belongs in Your Network
Eight	Potential Stories to Bring
Nine	After the Event
Ten	Grow & Nurture Your Network
Eleven	Final Thoughts
Twelve	Cheat Sheet
Resources	Organizations & Societies
Resources	Books

Why Networking is Important

Networking is one of the most critical skills for professionals, yet it is a soft skill that is rarely taught. Most of us are networking constantly – at work, at our kid's soccer games, at family events. We just don't call it networking.

Networking in the context of this guide is all about meeting people and maintaining regular contact with the ones that can help us or our companies. Most people generally understand the concept of networking, but the thought of going to a networking event is sometimes horrifying! Or, perhaps we're not scared, but we really don't have the right tools or understand how to make the time spent at such an event valuable to our jobs or our companies.

Within a business environment, networking happens in many places:

- Chamber of Commerce events
- Rotary clubs
- Conferences
- Trade shows
- Community non-profit organizations
- Professional society programs
- Client organization programs
- Tip groups

But why, exactly, would you want to network?

Find Project Opportunities

I've heard it stated that "Networking is the new business development," and couldn't agree more. Cold calling can be highly ineffective (especially for seller-doers). Traditional advertising and direct mail are less effective than they used to be. It's getting harder and harder to meet with prospective clients. However, if you can meet someone on "neutral territory," you won't be perceived as "someone trying to sell something," and a relationship can develop.

Meet Decision Makers

Networking allows you to meet decision makers – but not every time. You have to determine the place(s) where a decision-maker will be and find an excuse to attend!

Meet "Connectors" & "Influencers"

You'll often meet "connectors" or "influencers," and this is one of the great values of networking. A "connector" is someone who can introduce you to someone else that should be in your network. An "influencer" is someone who has the ability to exert some level of influence over a decision-maker. For instance, a facility manager may not be the ultimate decision-maker when it comes to selecting an A/E/C firm or team, but they may have a lot of influence in making recommendations to the final decision makers. Think of the "Six Degrees of Kevin Bacon"! Allegedly, Kevin can be connected to every other actor in Hollywood within six steps. This is really the concept behind a social networking site like LinkedIn – most of us are only a degree or two of separation from someone we want to know.

Meet Peers & Competitors

Depending upon the venue, you may be able to meet new peers in the industry, and there is nothing wrong with meeting and speaking with competitors. Remember, a competitor today may be a teammate tomorrow – and they could even refer work your way. Furthermore, someone working for a competitor may be a candidate to work for your firm in the future.

It's also good to have a "support group" – peers who are experiencing the same issues or challenges that you regularly face. For more than 25 years I've been a member of SMPS – the Society for Marketing Professional Services. Here I've met hundreds of peers. Sure, a few are competitors, but they are also friends. However, the vast majority are not competitors, and many have even become teammates or helped me along the way. I've joked countless times that SMPS really stands for **S**upport for **M**arketers of **P**rofessional **S**ervices – it's a tough industry, and it's just good to have a network of professional marketers and business developers to talk shop with!

Learn Trends

One of the most valuable things I've found about networking is the wealth of information that comes from conversations. I truly believe that the greatest benefit of attending a conference or professional society meeting is not the presentations themselves, but the conversations with others that you have before and after the presentations. You'll find out a lot about what is happening in the profession or industry. You'll learn about current or forthcoming trends. And you'll see these trends "in action" by hearing about how firms are dealing with them.

Gain Competitive Intelligence

Competitive intelligence is information that can help you gain a competitive advantage, whether it is better positioning your company to do business with a client or differentiating your company from the competition. Once you build a vibrant network and spend time at networking functions, you'll be surprised by how much you'll learn. I once was talking with a competitor, and he gave me the dirt on his firm! It's like he said, "Hey, do you want to know what our Achilles Heel is?" That, of course, is not common, but crazy things can happen during conversations. More likely, you'll get a few crumbs that you can leverage into a competitive advantage.

Identify Potential Hires

Networking is recruiting. When your company attends career fairs, the conversations are largely superficial. However, when you network, you can develop relationships with people that may fit well within your firm's corporate culture or help you meet strategic goals; in effect, you are able to pre-screen candidates. Just talk with your HR department about the quality of candidates they are getting from the company website or online job postings. Successful firms are filling their talent piplines by leveraging their networks, not by placing Help Wanted ads.

Career Fallback

None of us want to be downsized or rightsized; however, if it does happen, you will be able to use your network to find new career opportunities. The more robust your network, the quicker the path to your next job.

What Networking Is & Isn't

There's a lot of misinformation about networking – often spread by people who are poor networkers or who are scared of networking, so they make up "fake news" about it!

Networking is Connecting, not Collecting

He who dies with the most business cards does not win, so don't worry about collecting ten business cards at an event. The card itself is meaningless unless you have connected with the person who gave it to you. And just because you have a card and had a great conversation, that doesn't mean the person belongs in your network. The goal for networking is to make connections with people who can help you – and whom you can help.

Networking is Foundation Building

Networking isn't about sales, and it isn't about making superficial relationships. In fact, selling within a networking environment is so off-putting that it can bury a relationship before it even begins. Networking is about laying the foundations for future, mutually-beneficial relationships. The first step to constructing a new building is laying the foundation (well, after design, regulatory approvals, and site grading, but you get the metaphor!). Think about networking in that context. When you meet someone that may be a good fit for your network, focus on building strong foundations. Don't try to start by building walls or the roof before you have that sound foundation created.

Networking is Building Trust

This is critical. People do business with people they like and trust, and relationships can be developed through a series of networking contacts. If I meet you at an event tonight, and you try to sell me something tomorrow, the trust will be gone. In the early stages of any relationship, you get to know one-

another, building rapport and ultimately earning trust. No good will result if you can't build trust – or betray that trust.

Networking is Giving

This is a theme throughout the book. Networking is about giving, not getting. When you give, you develop trust. When you give, you become a valuable resource. When you give, you develop relationships faster. If you go into a networking relationship with a "What's in it for me?" attitude, the answer will be, "Nothing." Ultimately you will get a lot out of your relationships, but focus on the giving side of the equation first.

Networking is Not Schmoozing

Some people still think of networking as something that greasy salespeople do. The reality is that networking is about relationships and trust. Sure, there are also a few old-school schmoozers at any event. But people avoid them. Instead, they focus on meaningful introductions and conversations.

Networking is Not "Drinks with Friends"

Just as networking is not schmoozing, it is not all about wining and dining. True, many networking functions have food and beverage, but their presence is irrelevant to the purpose of networking. However, this is certainly a persistent stereotype.

Networking is Not Instant Business

When people downplay the value of networking, they'll often say, "I didn't get any leads." Really? Did you actually expect to get a lead from someone you just met? Relationships developed via networking provide value over years and decades – not the morning after.

Quality is Far Superior to Quantity

As I stated previously, networking should never be a quest to collect business cards. People who do this – or have a goal to come back with ten cards – often reach their quota of useless cards and leave, because they can check that off their list. Quality conversations trump the number of conversations you have, over and over and over again. Going to a networking event and having two or three meaningful conversations is better than meeting 30 people that you know nothing about – and who know nothing about you. What does this accomplish?

Networking is for Everyone

You do not have to be an extrovert to network, and the reality is that introverts and ambiverts (aka centroverts) may actually be better networkers than extroverts.

Extroverts Like to Talk

We all know the extroverts. They are gregarious, and often fun. But sometimes they are too loud or dominate the conversation, and often use "I" and "me" more than "you." Extroverts recharge through social activities and conversation, and often "think aloud." They love networking, but can be easily distracted by shiny objects. More than half of the US population are extroverts. Don't get me wrong – some of the best networkers I know are extroverts. But they also want to "work the room" and talk, if only briefly, with everyone. So their conversations may not be as in depth when compared to other personality types.

Introverts Would Rather Ask Questions Than Talk About Themselves

In the A/E/C industry, many technical professionals are introverts. It's common in this field. If you would rather work at your desk than talk with others, you are an introvert. If you would rather communicate with written words than have a conversation, you are an introvert. If you get recharged from working alone, you are an introvert. The great thing about introverts, however, is that they know how to ask questions and then listen to the answers. That is a critical skill for engineering, architecture, project management, and construction management. To do your job effectively, you have to know how to ask the right questions – and then shut up to focus on the answer. This is an equally critical skill for networking.

Ambiverts are Able to Balance Extrovert & Introvert Behaviors

Ambivert is a newer classification and refers to one who has both introvert and extrovert tendencies. When I took the Myers-Briggs test many years ago, I was a perfectly split between introvert and extrovert scores. In fact, I scored one point more in the introvert category, but the instructor moved me to the extrovert category for my personality type (ENTP) because I was outgoing at the program sessions. The reality is that I'm both. Some days I really enjoy networking with strangers – and I certainly love to get up in front of a group of people and present. However, I also get energized from alone time, a hallmark of an introvert.

In the networking world, ambivert is a great personality trait, combining the ability to question and listen with the fearlessness of talking with strangers!

Who Belongs In Your Network?

It's important to distinguish between networks and networking.

Your network comprises those people with whom you have a mutually trusting, beneficial relationship. It's a large, but not huge group. It's people that you want to help – and people that want to help you. With members of your network, you can have meaningful conversations, share opportunities, refer one-another, and do business.

Clients

Some of your clients belong in your network. But not all. Just because you have a very successful project does not mean that the client you worked with should be in your network. Remember that a network is a two-way street. Can you help them? Can they help you? Perhaps you have a quality relationship and want to keep them in your network. They may be able to write testimonials, serve as a reference, or refer potential clients or employees your way. Additionally, there may also be more work forthcoming, so you need to maintain regular contact – assuming they are a good client to work with and pay their bills! So how do you "give" to a client? Do quality work. Make them look good. Don't nickel and dime them for everything. Give them an occasional bit of free service (like helping them with a project budget) or a discount on fees.

Former Clients

Sometimes projects end and there are no new opportunities in the pipeline – but the relationship you developed during the project was great, and it makes sense to maintain the relationship after project completion. You never know what it will lead to down the road. Again, they can refer potential clients your way and, in the future, may have an opportunity to collaborate on a project again. Furthermore, the average tenure in a job in the US is less than five years (source: US Census Bureau), so your contact may very well be moving on to a different organization soon and will have new opportunities for you and your firm.

Potential Clients

Networking is a great business development tool, and through the process you may develop relationships with potential clients. It doesn't mean that you'll work with them on a project tomorrow, but it does lay a strong foundation for future work together. Not all potential clients belong in your network – what do you have to offer them? What do they have to offer you?

Vendors

In our industry, vendors represent a critical but underutilized network. Vendors have their ears to the ground and have much potential intelligence to share. Furthermore, they can open doors with potential clients and recommend prospective employees. In turn, you can specify their product, hire them for a service, or refer them to potential clients.

Co-Workers (Including at Other Offices)

Yes, your co-workers are part of your network. But just because you work with someone does not automatically put them in your network or you in their network. Remember that networking is a two-way street: how can you help one-another? If your firm has multiple offices, you may have co-workers at different locations – in different geographic regions – that are part of your network.

Former Co-Workers

Some of us have maintained relationships with people we used to work with – either at the companies we left or colleagues who are no longer working at our firms. These are valuable network contacts who often have deep relationships with us.

Community & Business Leaders

It's very important to have a network that includes leaders within the community, whether it be with organizations like United Way or the Boy Scouts as well as business organizations like chambers of commerce and economic development corporations. These people tend to be well-known and well-respected, have very broad networks themselves, can be both connectors and influencers, and may even potential clients.

Professional Association Contacts

I've been fortunate to be heavily involved with the Society for Marketing Professional Services at the national level, and have developed a great network of A/E/C contacts throughout the country. When you consider that a significant percentage of my firm's project opportunities come through other A/E/C firms, this is a great bonus! Your professional association contacts can provide advice, introduce you to others, be potential future hires, share "war stories" with you, and provide competitive intelligence. Don't overlook this segment of networking.

College Alumni

Professionals that you went to college with may also be part of your network, and if you are active with a college alumni association, you may find other individuals, that you didn't know in college, that belong in your network.

Personal Friends

Most of your friends belong in your friend network – not your business network. But you probably have a few friends that you can help from a business sense – and want to help you as well. These are the friends that should be part of your business network, so long as you have something to offer them.

Family Members

The same thing applies when it comes to family. Most of your family doesn't belong in your business network. But a select few members may be a valuable part of your network, so make sure to include them.

Former Network Members

Networks are in a constant state of change, and there may be a few former network members who you've grown out of touch with. Maybe they switched jobs and it no longer made sense to maintain regular contact, or whatever the case may be. But perhaps they've moved back into a position to connect, influence, or directly award work. It's time to reach out and get them back into your network.

Parents of Children's Friends – or Friends of Children

This is an often overlooked, yet valuable source of potential network contacts. If you have younger children, what do their friends' parents do? Or maybe you're a soccer coach, and it's your kid's teammate's father or mother. They may be an important connector, influencer, or even decision-maker. A former coworker of mine was a soccer coach, and one of the players on his team happened to be the child of an executive for a *Fortune 500* company. The relationship they developed more than two decades ago continues to bear fruit, as we've been working with that firm nonstop since the friendship was forged on the soccer field!

Although we all would love to stop aging in its tracks, we continue to age. When our children aren't children anymore, they develop their own networks. And a few people in their networks might be ideal candidates for our networks. The point is that your next great networking contact can come from anywhere!

Before the Event

Now that you understand networks and the myriad locations to find people that could potentially belong in your network, it's time to turn our attention to the dreaded networking event. These events come in all shapes and sizes: networking-specific events, time devoted to networking before or after an educational program, trade shows, conferences, service clubs, business organizations, professional societies, and the list goes on.

Regardless of the venue, you know you will be networking. Just like you should warm up before that next golf game or tennis match, or prepare before that next business meeting, there are some networking "warm up" tips that can help make your networking event a positive experience.

Know Why You Are Going (Or Not Going)

Before you head to a networking event, you must first ask yourself a simple question: "Why am I going?"

Roughly a kazillion hours are wasted annually by people attending networking events for no reason other than to "look busy."

There are few assets more valuable than your time, so protect it carefully. Think about the Return On Investment for attending a program, conference, or networking event. There's always an opportunity cost to be paid; that is, the "cost" of not doing something else, the forfeited opportunity left undone because you chose to attend an event. It could be working on a project, writing a proposal, meeting with a client, reaching out to potential or former clients, updating specification masters, educating yourself on a new product or approach, or any one of hundreds of other things. All these activities have a value, too.

There are so many potential places to network – chamber of commerce events, conferences, trade shows, client association meetings, professional society meetings, service clubs, etc. – that you could probably find a networking event to attend every single day of the week most weeks of the year!

Before you decide to go, determine what you are trying to get out of it. There are myriad reasons to attend, which were covered in the first chapter.

Once you know why you are going, next determine if it is the right venue to meet your goals. Maybe it is, but maybe it isn't. Don't go to just fill space. Don't go just so you can demonstrate that you were "networking." Go with a purpose!

Conversely, don't **not** go because you are "too busy." Everyone has pressing deadlines. Everyone is just as busy as you think you are. So the "too busy" excuse is really nothing more than that: an excuse. For every kazillion hours wasted by people attending events for no real reason, another kazillion hours of quality networking are missed because people didn't take the initiative to attend, or used the lame "too busy" excuse to justify not going. Just think of all the missed connections, relationships, project opportunities, and amazing-potential-employees-who-will-never-be.

The benefits of networking are very real, but only if the venue is a match for your goals. Pick the right place for the right reasons to increase your odds of networking success!

Organize Your Business Cards

It seems obvious that you should take business cards to a networking event, yet it is amazing how many times I see people go to meetings or events and say, "I forgot to bring my cards!" Don't be this person!

But what does it mean to organize your business cards? I like to have two storage areas for business cards. If I'm wearing a suit coat, it is easy – one pocket is for my business cards to give out, and another pocket is for any business card I receive. Of course, this only works if you have pockets!

Some people carry business card cases, and keep their cards in the front, then place cards they receive in the back. Sometimes your nametag, particularly at a conference, can serve as a storage area – or even a special pocket in your purse.

Just as you should never be on a quest to collect business cards, you also shouldn't force your card into the hands of someone you just met. Networking is about connecting, and in many cases there will be no need to exchange cards with someone you are meeting for the first time. We all have piles of business cards from people we can't remember – we don't know where or when we met them, and couldn't pick them out of a police line-up to save our lives … so why did we exchange cards in the first place?

Know How to Wear Your Nametag

Believe it or not, there's a correct place for your nametag! It belongs on your right side, chest level, so when someone shakes your hand it is easy for them to see.

You'll often get a nametag when you check in at an event. Many times the tag will be disposable with adhesive on back – stick it on when you arrive, peel it and pitch it on your way out the door. Other times, the nametag will have a pin or clip on the back, making it easy to place on a jacket, but not so easy for a shirt or a dress.

Professional networkers know the value of a permanent nametag – something that has a company logo and their name on it, often with a magnet on the back. These only cost a few bucks and can make you look more professional.

However, sometimes the provided tags have important information on them, so you need to wear them or keep them handy – the nametag may be needed to get you through the door or into a certain room.

At conventions and conferences, you often receive a nametag on a lanyard. It might have a code or ribbon on it. Use that one instead of your company tag, or consider wearing both.

Know How to Shake Hands

Schools should teach proper handshakes from the earliest years of study. Many adults have no clue how to shake a hand, and something as simple as a handshake can leave a positive, or negative, impression.

Your handshake should be firm, but not overpowering. Some people squeeze so hard if feels like they are crushing the bones in your hand. Conversely, avoid the dreaded "limp fish" handshake, where your hand feels like a dead fish. That's very awkward for both parties.

One or two pumps is all that is needed. Some people get carried away with the pumps – too much motion, too fast.

Beware the premature clasp, where you reach out to shake someone's hand, and end up squeezing their fingers. No one likes to be on the receiving end of that maneuver.

If you know the person well, it's okay to hold their hand a bit longer, or even bring in a second hand for the "double handshake." This is best left for close friends and contacts. Otherwise, don't linger in the handshake for too long, because that's just creepy!

As silly as it seems, it's okay to practice your handshake if you're not comfortable with your technique! And by all means, if you work with someone with a bad handshake, advise them so they don't continue to embarrass themselves!

Wear Proper Attire

It's always important to know your audience and the forum, so dress appropriately. This does not always mean that you should be wearing a suit or skirt. The general rule is to dress like others will be dressing, but if you don't know, err on side of overdressing. A suit coat or tie could always be removed, if need be.

I once went to a conference, and a colleague told me in advance that it would be extremely casual. Because it took place over the summer, I packed my uniform: polo shirts and khakis. However, the first day I realized that the conference was business casual, and I was underdressed. Fortunately there was a department store a few blocks from my hotel, so I ran out and purchased a couple of dress shirts and tee shirts. Now, I almost always wear dress shirts – I can always roll up my sleeves! I also travel with one or two sport coats, in case I need them.

Know Your Audience

Speaking of knowing your audience, think about the specific event you plan to attend, and the type of people that will be there. Are they executives? Design professionals? Construction managers? Facilities managers? General business people? Community leaders? Colleagues?

You'll need stories and questions that are relatable to the people you will be meeting with, so try to determine that in advance.

Find Out Who Will be Attending

One of the best ways to do this is to obtain a list of registered attendees, if possible. Some organizations post this information online prior to an event, or even send an email with the information to registered attendees. If you don't receive or gain access to a list, it's okay to reach out to the meeting organizer. They might be willing to share that information – but that's not always the case.

If you can see who is coming, you can develop a plan of action for seeking out key contacts beforehand, and know to look for them at the event. You might also be able to determine a connector or influencer that can introduce you to someone you want to meet, so make plans to do this in advance. You can also reach out to your existing network to see who regularly attends the meeting / conference / event you are going to. Or even post on LinkedIn that you are planning to attend and ask who else is going.

Come Equipped with Questions to Ask

We are going to go over this in much more detail later in the book, but it is important to pre-plan some boilerplate questions – as well as a specific question or two for a key contact you are hoping to meet. It is important to get to know people, so getting others talking and keeping the conversation flowing can be accomplished with good questions.

Come Equipped with Stories to Share

Likewise, you'll need to pre-plan a few anecdotes. Target your stories to the audience if you can, and then have a few generic stories that can be shared with anyone. Again, we'll cover story ideas later in the book, but it is critical to have several interesting things to share, both to engage the people you are speaking with, as well as to keep the conversation flowing. Avoid awkward silence!

Prepare Three "Speeches": About You, About Your Role, About Your Company

You've heard it called the elevator speech, 15-second commercial, or 30-second commercial. This is really a personal brand statement – a spoken sentence or two to answer a question asked of you.

The question can take three forms:

1. Tell me about yourself. (Who are you?)
2. What do you do at your company? (What is your role?)
3. What can you tell me about your company? (What does your company do?)

Personally, I believe the best elevator speech ever written is actually more of a question to get the other person talking: "Tell me about yourself." However, the reality is that you will be getting the question, so you need to be prepared. You can have boring boilerplate responses, which is the most common approach, or say something a bit more interesting to hopefully further the conversation.

About You

> "Hi. I'm Scott Butcher with JDB Engineering in York, Pennsylvania. I oversee the sales and marketing programs by day, and research, write, and photograph books as a hobby."

This is a basic response to answer the question "Who are you?" It may be effective, but it is boring and unmemorable.

> "Hi. I'm Scott Butcher with JDB Engineering in York, Pennsylvania. Day or night, I'm always researching or writing – either to generate new business for my company or for one of the fifteen books that I've written."

Here's a variation of the original response that is a bit more lively. The key is that I want to give a broad answer that covers my work and non-work lives. You could just as easily say, "Married for 25 years and proud parent of two kids." The canned answer is always, "Hi, I'm Bob, and I'm an architect with Acme Design." This is uttered hundreds of times at A/E/C networking events, and is a waste of your breath! You are more than your job, so share something interesting about yourself.

About Your Role

> "Hi. I'm Scott Butcher. I'm vice president of JDB Engineering, overseeing the sales and marketing functions for a full-service engineering firm."

Next up is the answer to "What do you do?" Here's a boilerplate response and again, it answers the question, but totally lacks pizzazz.

> "Hi. I'm Scott Butcher. I'm vice president of JDB Engineering. My role is to continually look 'around the corner' for the next opportunity, and to make sure we effectively respond to those that make the most sense for our company."

A slight rewrite can make you sound a little more interesting while not seeming quite as canned. It can be even more engaging:

"Hi. I'm Scott Butcher with JDB Engineering. Have you ever read a blog by an engineer or attended a presentation given by one? I regularly work with engineers to make them better writers and public speakers!"

About Your Company

"Hi. I'm Scott Butcher with JDB Engineering. We provide engineering solutions for industrial, institutional, and mixed-use clients."

Finally, this is a response to the query, "What does your company do?" Sometimes a geographic region can be added, like "… along the East Coast." This response works, but rather boringly so!

"Hi. I'm Scott Butcher with JDB Engineering. We provide design and construction solutions to help our clients make their stuff better – whether it's manufacturing motorcycles, producing chocolate bars, or providing a better learning environment for students!"

This is far more interesting, isn't it? And it can actually be a conversation starter: "Motorcycles? Chocolate bars? Tell me about that…"

Best / Test

There are a number of quality networking books available. *Making Your Contacts Count* is published by the American Management Association. The authors propose a two-step answer to the question, "What do you do?" They call it Best/Test.

The first part of your response would be your primary talent – what you do best, like engineering, project management, or basket-weaving.

The second part is a self-testimonial – in other words, some sort of evidence that your "best" is true. This is where you can share about how you served a client or saved the day.

"I was on the engineering team that figured out how to build a theater nine feet away from the New York subway system. We did it without interfering with any of the rehearsals and performances going on directly above us in Carnegie Hall."

This example of Best/Test for an engineer is taken directly from the book.

I tend to view this as a great story to share, perhaps deeper into the conversation. I don't know what type of engineer the person is, or where he or she works. In fact, I don't even know the person's role on the project, so more detail is needed.

The most important thing is to be comfortable when you answer. If anything beyond 'boring' makes you squeamish, stick with the boring – but at least say it with some enthusiasm!

Or, if you feel comfortable doing so, get creative with your response!

Know Thyself

Have you ever asked a person something about themselves and they had to think, or started with "Uh, um..."

Like, "Where did you go to college?"

"College? Uh ... um ... Penn State."

You'd think it would be on the tip of their tongue, right?

As it turns out, a lot of people don't feel comfortable talking about themselves. They were brought up to "not brag," and talking about themselves feels like bragging. But in this context, it really isn't!

The questions that follow are ones you should be able to answer instantly. Furthermore, many of these questions are also effective in driving a networking conversation, where you take the role of the questioner.

Without a doubt, if you are at a networking event you will be asked a few questions. Some will be about your professional persona, while others will be about your personal side.

To borrow the Boy Scout motto: when it comes to networking, it's always best to "Be Prepared." So be prepared to *answer and ask* these questions, as appropriate:

What do You Do?

You have a title. You also have a role, which might be different than your title. In fact, you may have multiple roles. And then there are your responsibilities that go along with each role. The top executive of your firm may be president or CEO. That's his or her title.

But the roles are myriad:

- Executive
- Project Manager
- Business Developer
- Engineer or architect or CM
- Mentor

And with each of these roles, he or she has different responsibilities.

What is your title and your role? This relates to the elevator speeches we covered, but can go deeper than that 15-second speech.

What are Your Hobbies? (What do You do for Fun?)

What gets your juices flowing when not at work? (Or, to be honest: at work!) Reading or watching movies? Golf? Wood-working or quilting? Birding? Writing? PTO? Coaching your kids' sports teams?

Everyone has a life outside of work. What's yours?

What is Your Education & Experience?

You might be asked about your educational background.

Where did you go to school? Usually this means college, but not always, particularly if you're at a smaller, local function like a chamber of commerce event, Rotary Club meeting, etc., where the questioner is trying to determine if you grew up in the area and any potential local mutual acquaintances you may have.

How long have you been in the business? This is another common question. You don't have to be specific. I just say "more than two decades." You can be even more vague … "Long enough to become an expert." Or, "Long enough to remember drafting boards."

What Are Your Proudest Accomplishments?

How about your accomplishments? This is another question you may be asked at a networking function, although not necessarily in those exact terms.

It may be, "What's the coolest project you've worked on?" Or, "What is one thing that really stands out in your career?"

But the question could also apply to your non-work life.

Maybe it is your spouse and kids. Maybe it is coaching your kid's team of soccer misfits to the league championship. Maybe it is completing Tough Mudder.

What Does Your Spouse / Partner / Significant Other Do?

I get this one a lot. "So what does your wife do?"

For me, I answer that one with a short story:

"Well, she was the communications director for a community foundation when our son was born. Of course, he decided to arrive 14 weeks early and only weighed 1-pound, 3-ounces, so he lived in the NICU for four months. Because he spent most of his time on a ventilator, and went home still on oxygen, the doctors strongly suggested that he not be sent to daycare or to a babysitter, so either my wife or I needed to quit our jobs. I volunteered, but lost! So my wife, Debbie, left her job to stay home with him. He's thriving, doing well in school, and playing baseball! Of course, even though he's getting older, my wife still says 'I don't have to go back to work, do I?'"

I usually add that she is as busy as I am with her nonprofit and volunteer teaching activities! That's certainly a more interesting response than "Stay-at-home mom."

I always end with a smile. People love that story – everyone knows someone touched by prematurity. They often ask questions about my son or the NICU experience. And it just so happens that several people in my network have been personally affected by prematurity in their family, and in a few cases it was the shared experience that originally connected us.

What Activities are Your Children Involved With?

If you want to connect with a person, ask about their children. This is an old sales adage, but really comes into play in networking.

Once people find out that you have kids, they will often ask about their ages, their activities, their school district, etc. Give information freely, but also know that they are dying to tell you about their children as well, so make sure you ask a reciprocal question about their kids!

What are You Passionate About?

Have you ever really sat down and thought about what you are most passionate about? Or about what inspires you? How would you answer these questions?

Think about it, because not only is it a potential question you might hear at a networking event, but it can also help you develop some of the stories that define who you are.

What are Your Goals – or What is on Your Bucket List?

The goals question is more common, but a bucket-list question is a way to keep things light.

The goal question may be, "So do you hope to take over the company one day?" Or, "What's next for you in this profession?"

Sometimes if the question is more general, "What are your goals?", that's a chance to segue into 'bucket list.' "Well, I'd like to spend Oktoberfest in Munich!" or, "Actually, my kids are getting older, so I'm looking forward to getting more involved with several nonprofit organizations."

Where Are Your From?

This question is fairly common, particularly at events with people coming from a large geographic region.

Nametags will often have city and state listed, so a typical question asked of me is: "Where exactly is York, Pennsylvania?"

I always answer so people from other parts of the country can understand: "We're about 50 miles north of Baltimore and 75 miles west of Philadelphia" or, "We're sandwiched between the Gettysburg battlefield, Lancaster Amish community, and Hershey – the sweetest place on earth." If your location is not everyday knowledge, make it relatable.

Of course, if your nametag says, "New York, NY," people will probably ask if you work in Manhattan.

What is Interesting About You or Your Family?

This is yet another potential question that you might have to think about, but one that won't necessarily be asked in those exact terms. My wife has one of the best answers I ever heard, and I've stolen it and used it many times (like I am now!):

Her dad is Tom Green. Tom's first wife was named Black. They divorced. His ex-wife married a man named Ruby. Tom then married a woman named Brown.

But it gets better.

When my wife was at Kutztown University of Pennsylvania, she was Miss Berks County. This was when a new Crayola Crayon factory opened in nearby Easton, Pennsylvania, and because her last name was Green, she was invited to be a participant in a parade to celebrate the grand opening. When she finished the parade route, Jeanne Moos from CNN ran up to her with camera in tow, put a microphone in her face, and asked: "Do you have any interesting color stories?"

Debbie shared that story.

More than a thousand miles away in Naples, FL, her godparents were sitting in a diner, eating. A TV was playing in the background. Her godmother heard something familiar and said, "Wait, I know that voice ..." and sure enough, when they looked at the TV, there was Debbie telling her color story. Alas, their last name was not a color!

What Differentiates Your Firm from the Competition?

You regularly attend networking functions, whether you realize it or not: PTOs, kids sports and scouting, school board meetings, nonprofit organization get-togethers, etc.

No matter where you are, you should always be thinking about your network as it applies to business. Whether a personal or business-related event, you'll invariably get asked about your company. Sometimes you can give a simple answer like we covered previously, but it is always important to know why your company is different than other firms offering the same services.

We're talking differentiation here, and your company should provide you with talking points. How do you articulate your brand? What makes your firm different from every other firm that operates in the same geographic or vertical markets?

During the Event

You've completed practice, and the time of the big game is upon you!

Here are some tips – from the time you arrive throughout your networking experience:

Put Your Day Neatly Away in a Box

You've got deadlines to meet. Mistakes to correct. Clients waiting for your call. A significant other not happy that you'll be home late tonight. Or any one of a million other stress-inducing things.

But guess what? You need to put them away in a box for the hour or two you are networking. I promise that they will still be there for you after the networking is over! I can also personally guarantee that no one will steal your "box"! We all have our own boxes.

It is imperative that you be in the right frame of mind to network, or you won't have success. Your time will have been wasted – as will have the time of those you spoke with.

Get Energized!

Basically, you need positive energy, and you need to have it before you walk in the door. No one wants to network with Negative Nellie!

How do you get yourself pumped up for other things? Do you give yourself a pep talk? Do you call someone and have them give you a pep talk?

Do you listen to certain music?

Music is actually a great technique. Have you ever attended a conference with a keynote speaker? What's happening as people arrive prior to the keynote? Music is blaring! And it's never a ballad, is it?

Likewise, have you ever been to a rock concert? Is it silent when people arrive? No, music plays right up until the band is introduced.

In both cases the purpose is to pump up the audience, to get them in the right frame of mind. You need to do whatever it takes to get your head in the right frame of mind before you walk through the door.

For me, a bit of AC/DC's "Back in Black" usually does the trick!

When You First Arrive

You've arrived, but you're not ready to mingle just yet.

Here's what you need to do before you hit the registration desk: go find a mirror, probably in a rest room. Double check your appearance. Are you neat or disheveled? Step up close to the mirror and smile. What's in your teeth? Hopefully not your lunch!

"Brush Your Breath"

Do you remember that old commercial for Dentyne gum? That's what you need to do: brush your breath. Chew gum on the way. Suck a mint as you arrive. Brush your teeth before you leave the office, home, or hotel room. Whatever. Just don't have bad breath (or its sibling, body odor), because that is what people will remember! No amount of charm will overcome dragon breath or "Pig Pen" body odor!

Arrive Early

They say never be first to a party, so why would you want to be one of the first people at a networking event? For starters, you'll be able to get a lay of the land much easier without a lot of bodies in the way.

More importantly, it is easier to engage in conversation. There will only be a handful of people, and you'll be able to easily approach a few people who are not yet engaged in a discussion. If networking makes you nervous, this is an especially effective tactic.

Check the Nametag Table to See Who Has Yet to Arrive

Your first networking interaction at an event will probably be with those at the registration table – if there is not a line behind you, engage those at the table in conversation.

Also check out the tags. If you've seen a list of attendees in advance, you'll be able to determine who is already there – particularly if it is someone you want to speak with.

If you haven't seen a list, this is how you can determine who else is attending. As you look over the nametags, make a mental list of people you want to connect with during the event.

Don't Stress – Take a Few Deep Breaths

This truly works. While networking is not as high on the list of human fears as public speaking, spiders, and snakes, a lot of people are still scared by it.

There's no reason for this! You've talked with strangers the first day on the job, at project meetings, at PTO meetings, at parties, at nonprofit functions, etc. This is no different!

"Fight or flight" drains blood from your brain, and makes it difficult to think straight ... and this is a natural response to networking for people that don't do it often. So how do you regain your mental equilibrium? It's just this simple: take several deep breaths.

Remember the Platinum Rule

Forget about the Golden Rule. Don't treat others as you want to be treated. Instead, follow the Platinum Rule: Treat others as they want to be treated.

This is a simple, great rule for any relationship – including those developed during networking. Through the course of a networking conversation, you'll learn things about your conversation partner. Make mental notes, which will help you understand how they want to be treated during future conversations.

At the most basic, ask what name they would like to be called. "William, do you prefer Bill?"

Or how their name is pronounced: "I apologize for asking this, but can you tell me again how your name is pronounced? People often say 'Boo-ker' instead of 'Butcher,' and I don't want to make that mistake with you."

Qualify the Person

You will meet a lot of people through the course of an event or many events over a year. But just because you met someone doesn't mean they belong in your network. Make a determination if they belong in your network or not, because if they do, you'll want to further the conversation with them and if they don't, maybe it's time to move on.

Hang Out by the: Entrance, Bar, or Food

Here's another great technique for meeting people: stand close to the game trails.

There are three obvious game trails during the hunt. First, people must enter a room from somewhere, right? Hang near the registration table, but not close enough to cause a back-up should you engage in conversation.

Second, there's always a good line at the bar – especially if there is a free drink or two involved! Stand where people are passing by as they go to get their drinks or leave with drinks in hand. I've been at a networking event, planted myself near the bar, and barely moved for more than 60 minutes because I had a number of meaningful conversations with people coming or going.

Third, hang near the food table. Stand along one of the paths that people are taking to get to the food – but try to get them before they have food in hand. Once they have it, they are going to want to eat, not talk with you (unless you also have food and join them at a table).

Get in a Line

People hate lines. Lines are boring. So what do we do in lines? We talk with the person in front of us or turn around and talk with the person behind us.

This is a great way to start a conversation. Often you'll talk with someone in the bar line, each get your drink, and then continue the conversation afterward. People in line are a captive audience!

Minimize Eating & Drinking

While it is good to hang by the food and beverage lines, think "minimization" when it comes to partaking in the offerings.

I rarely eat at evening networking events – if I have anything, it will be a piece or two of cheese or a cracker – something quick and not likely to stick in my teeth. Sometimes networking programs are for breakfast, lunch, or dinner, and eating is unavoidable. Just proceed with caution – make sure you don't eat messy foods.

Alcohol is a double-edged sword. On the positive side, it helps take the edge off. I know people who immediately go to the bar when they arrive at a networking event, simply because a few sips of wine calms their nerves!

However, you really need to watch how much you drink. Nurse your beer or wine – consider not getting anything heavier, even if it is available. Don't even get close to being tipsy or buzzed – and remember, by the time you think you are buzzed, others have been noticing it for quite a while.

Depending upon the type of event, I might limit myself to a single alcoholic beverage. But for other events with my "tribe" – hanging with a group that I know well, I may be a bit looser (but not a stumbling drunk, mind you!).

Note what others are drinking. If alcohol is available, but no one is partaking, don't be the first. If everyone is drinking wine, then don't drink beer – drink wine or soda or nothing at all.

There's a woman I see perhaps once a year at an industry event. She never doesn't have a glass of wine in her hand. She talks way too close to you and her breath always smells of alcohol. Everyone else calls her "chardonnay breath" behind her back. Don't be chardonnay breath!

Find a Standing-Only Table

This is actually a great technique if you are too nervous to approach someone to start a conversation.

A lot of networking events have high-top café tables but no chairs. Grab your beverage – or piece of cheese – and head over to one of these tables. If one or two people are there, great. You have a reason to be at the table just like they do. Engage in conversation.

Do not let yourself get stressed about approaching a partially-occupied table. Simply ask if you may join the person or people already there.

If the table is empty, hold tight. As people arrive, someone is bound to get food and come join you. Engage in conversation. Also, be polite and give up your spot if you don't need it and someone with a full plate approaches the table.

Scan the Room

Early in the networking session, scan the room to get the layout and determine who is already there.

As you get some 'downtime' between conversations, scan the room again. Who else has arrived? Was there someone you wanted to speak with who was engaged in conversation at the time? Are they now available?

Seek Out Clients & Potential Clients

Depending upon the type of networking event, there may be existing or prospective clients.

Make sure you take the time to speak with them – even if you aren't on the project team.

That's such a perfect opener: "John? Hi, I'm Scott Butcher with JDB Engineering. My company is collaborating with you on the central plant project, and we really appreciate the opportunity to work with you…"

If you are not talking with them, your competitors sure will be!

Find the Lone Wolf

This is another tried and true technique.

There's always someone off to the side, feeling awkward and uncomfortable. Networking just isn't their "thing." They are there for a reason, but they just aren't sure what to do. In fact, their boss may have told them to attend!

Help alleviate their awkwardness. Approach them, smile, stick out your hand, and say "Hi." You will be making their day.

Know How to Join a Conversation

Many people feel very uncomfortable about joining a conversation that is in progress. It seems unnatural and even rude.

Remember, however, that you are at a networking event, and the whole purpose is to meet and talk with others – new connections or old acquaintances!

If two neighbors down the street were having a conversation in one's yard – and you didn't know either of them – would you approach and try to jump in? Probably not. But with networking, this is acceptable and expected. Here's three tried and true approaches:

Lurk & Listen

First, what I call the 'lurk & listen,' which entails approaching a group, standing a few feet away, and listening to the conversation. You want to get a feel for the discussion, and also listen for either an opening to jump in and introduce yourself, or a key conversation point to which you can add something interesting. This is not being rude, so long as you don't interrupt.

Tap Someone You Know

Second, if you know someone in the group, walk up and tap them – but not while they are talking, or being directly talked to. They will usually smile, reach out their hand, and step aside to let you into the group. Eye contact with a familiar face also works well.

Walk Up, Smile & Extend Your Hand

Finally, you can be very direct. Walk right up to a group having a conversation, wait for them to look at you, smile, extend your hand, and say, "Hi, Scott Butcher with JDB Engineering. This looks like the fun conversation! Mind if I tag in?"

Understand Open & Closed Conversations

Before joining a discussion, you need to pay attention to the type of conversation that is taking place.

If two (or more) people are standing closely together, facing one another, and talking in hushed voices, this is a closed conversation. They are talking about something very specific that involves them, and they are giving you the signal that they don't want to be approached right now. Respect the nonverbal clues.

Conversely, most networking conversations are open conversations. Two people talking are at an angle, not directly facing one another. Groups are standing at a position as to leave a 'hole' for someone else to enter. These conversations are very approachable, and offer the perfect opening for you.

Find a Wingman

The term "wingman" comes from the military, and in World War II referred to the secondary plane that would fly off to the side and slightly behind the main attack plane.

In *Top Gun*, Tom Cruise's character, Maverick, had a real problem playing the role of wingman.

Wingman is now often used in a social setting, and usually refers to two guys – the primary guy brings the wingman with him to help him meet girls. A lot of romantic comedy films employ use of a wingman – or wing-woman.

However, there's actually a networking connotation, but its definition is somewhat reversed. There are always people at networking events that seem to know everyone, and it's great to have them as your wingman. The reason I suggest it is "reversed" is because they are the primary, and you are the secondary person ... but you want to meet people, and you are relying on them to help make introductions.

Don't Only Talk with People You Know

It is absolutely acceptable to speak to people you know, and the easiest thing to do at a networking event. Just don't spend the entire time doing it.

Do ask if they can introduce you to anyone important who happens to be there. And determine if you can introduce anyone to them.

There's one organization I belong to and have a colleague that has become a good friend. We often walk around networking events together, but are frequently engaged in conversations with different people. If my conversation ends first, he'll invite me into his conversation, and vice-versa. Perhaps we're one-another's wingman!

Be a Listener

We have two ears and one mouth. So listen twice as much as you talk. This is the key to successful networking – how else are you going to find out about people and determine if they belong in your network? Earlier in this book we looked at the differences between extroverts, introverts, and ambiverts when it comes to networking. Extroverts often talk too much, which is why introverts have the ideal skills for networking.

Never Interrupt

This is just good manners, but there seems to be interrupters everywhere. Interrupters can be at the office or at home – and most certainly at networking events. I've been trying to help people, and they keep interrupting me! If I have information that could help you, but you won't let me tell you because of your loquaciousness, why would I want to continue to try to help you? Why would others?

Be Conservative with Business Cards

At I stated previously, it's not a race to see who can collect the most business cards.

If you're like most professionals, you have stacks of business cards with absolutely no connection to you. You don't remember who they are or where you met them. Sure, you've got tons of 'em, but is that effective networking?

Share cards with people that you think should belong in your network, then ask for theirs. Also get their cards if you believe they belong in someone else's network – and offer to make the introduction.

But don't walk around with a stack of cards in your hand, handing them to anyone who looks at you! That's considered a "worst practice" for networking! And it also creates the impression that you're just there to sell.

Take a Time Out

If you are not a regular networker – or even if you are – sometimes it makes sense to "take five."

Go to the restroom. Find a table to the side and sit down. Let your mind absorb and catch up. It's totally understandable: even professional athletes need to come out of the game for a breather every once in a while!

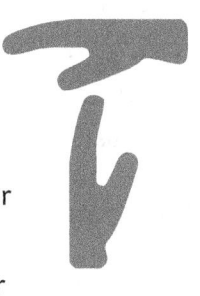

Don't Hide in a Corner, Playing on Your Smartphone to Look "Busy"

There's a difference between taking a break and just plain hiding.

Today's smartphones make it easy to hide while pretending to look important. You're not at a networking event to check email or browse the web. Don't get me wrong, you'll see a lot of people doing this. For some it is legit. But for many others, it is merely hiding.

Check your email during that five-minute break. Otherwise, forget you even have a smartphone with you – unless you are checking your calendar because one of your networking contacts has asked about your availability or you are looking up someone's number to share.

Share Liberally

We're going to cover this more in a bit, but networking is giving – sharing information, leads, contacts, and knowledge. With networking, you get to play the role of Santa Claus. Effective networking provides the gifts that keep on giving, so always be looking to help the people in your network.

Buy a Quality Contact a Drink

Some networking events will provide a single drink ticket – and honestly, this is probably all you'll need. But sometimes you'll be engaged in a really good conversation with a client, a prospective client, a connector, or someone who is providing valuable information. If your glasses are empty, and it seems that they are ready for a refill, go ahead and offer to buy. Most networking is Dutch treat, but occasionally it makes sense to buy a connection a drink.

Invite People into Conversations

There's few things more awkward than standing on a perimeter of a conversation, waiting for an invite to join, and never getting that invite. It's like being the uncool kid in school, watching the cool clique do fun things and carry on.

In networking, if you ever find yourself engaged in a conversation and someone is waiting to join, don't let them dangle in the wind: go ahead and smile, reach out your hand, and say hello. This is an offer to join. They'll remember your generosity.

Note Interesting Things that People are Wearing

At networking functions, you'll usually find one or two people that are dressed atypically, flashy, or generally loud. Maybe it is an extension of their personality (which means they will be a blast to talk with!), or maybe they just like to stand out from the crowd.

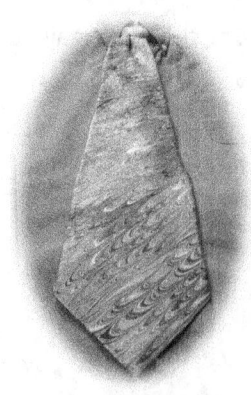

Comment on their attire. They'd love to hear a compliment. Don't say, "Wow, could you be any 'louder' with that outfit?" Rather, say: "You're looking colorful and cheery." Or that's a great watch … or ring … or tie … or whatever.

Take this tie for instance. Several years ago, my wife and I were in Williamsburg, Virginia, and happened to be there during an art show. Some artist was selling these crazy custom-made ties and scarves, and my wife picked this one out for me.

It's a little flashier than my typical boring ties (which I rarely wear these days, anyway), but I'm amazed how often people compliment this silly tie.

At first it was at the office. And then at networking events. Some guy once wanted to buy it off me at an event. I was in Philadelphia for a meeting, walking down Market Street, and a homeless woman walking past me said, "Hey – that's a great tie!"

I even wrote an ode to the tie on my ENR.com Marketropolis blog!

Compliment & Thank Others – But Don't go Overboard

This is a continuation of the previous tip, but remember that there are a lot of things you can compliment someone on.

If they are full of great stories, tell them. "Wow, that's a great story. Thank you for sharing it!"

If they share liberally, say "You are a fountain of knowledge and an excellent resource."

And be sure to thank them whenever they share with you. Say thank you during the conversation. Say thank you via an email or hand-written note after the event.

Ask About Accomplishments

People love to talk about their accomplishments. Sure, there are some blow-hards that will happily tell you about their latest accomplishment or, even worse, how much they make or how big their bonus was. Or they love name-dropping. My favorite example is a guy I know that name drops constantly; however, no one else knows who the heck he's talking about! We know he's kind of being a jerk, we just don't know to what extent!

While we like talking about our accomplishments, most of us are very guarded with what we say. We're too humble to risk coming across as braggards. We've been taught that it is rude. So how do you get someone to talk about their accomplishments? Simply ask.

Say, "Have any of your projects won awards?"

Or even more directly, "What's your proudest accomplishment?"

Also consider approaching it from a different angle: "What's the coolest project you've worked on?" "What is your craziest project experience?" These questions allow them to talk about a project instead of themselves, and yet you learn a lot about them through their stories.

Don't Ask for Free Advice – or Give Advice Unless Asked for It

This is an important component of networking etiquette.

Just because someone tells you they are a real estate agent doesn't give you license to probe them with questions about how you should stage your home for resale. Just because someone tells you that they sell life insurance doesn't mean you can turn that around and ask if the rate you are paying is too high – and certainly don't ask for tips about how to renegotiate, most likely with the person's competitor!

On the flip side, if someone does ask for advice, it's okay to offer it. As you get to know people in your network better, it will become increasingly acceptable to ask one-another for advice.

But if someone doesn't ask for your advice, don't give it. Unsolicited advice is worth the amount the recipient has paid for it.

Offer to Pass Along Information

Sometimes when you meet someone new, they will want immediate access to one of your contacts. But because this person is a new contact, you won't feel comfortable making an introduction just yet. That's totally acceptable, and if the new contact is bothered by this, they are violating a networking rule and really not worthy of being in your network. Everyone must have respect for their network connections.

Instead, just say "Why don't you give me your card and write on the back what information you're looking for, and I'll pass it along to him or her."

Sometimes your new contact won't ask, but you'll determine that they have information of value to someone in your network, or vice versa. In this case it is okay to make an offer to pass something along.

A lot of people won't be able to benefit you directly, but will be able to help someone in your network. As a networker, you need to keep your eyes peeled for this, and make sure you help other people in your network.

Listen with Your Mind

We already reviewed the importance of listening, but that was related to your eyes and ears – paying attention to the person speaking.

However, you can still be listening with your ears – but not with your mind!

When someone is talking to you, be sure you are listening with your mind and not focusing on what you will say next. You'll miss the conversation at best, and at worst appear disinterested. This focused approach is known as active listening.

Don't Look Around the Room for Someone Else to Speak With

Here's the extreme example of not listening: being so disinterested in a conversation that you actually look around the room to find someone else to talk with.

You feign engagement with an occasional, "Yup," or "Uh-huh," but it is quite obvious that you are bored.

Don't be one of those people distracted by shiny objects.

Don't be a Close-Talker

Here's another important not-to-do: close-talking. An entire episode of *Seinfeld* centered around a close-talker!

We've all been stuck talking with the close-talker, haven't we? In our society, a distance of three-feet between talkers is the cultural norm, closer if there is a lot of noise in the room.

But the close-talker doesn't respect this rule, nor your personal space. And if you take a step backward, what do they do?

Follow you! And do they ever have fresh breath?

Take Another Break

You know what? Sometimes during a long networking event, you need a second break ... maybe another mental time-out, or maybe simply because your legs are tired (so consider leaving those 4-inch heels at home when networking!). I've been to countless events that were held in large rooms or ballrooms, with couches or seating in the hallway. These spots make a great place to duck out for a few minutes – but often you'll encounter a few other people doing the same thing, and you'll end up striking up another conversation!

Make Eye Contact with Everyone

Don't walk around a room looking down. People want to meet and engage you, but eyes to the floor make this impossible. It also makes you unapproachable. If you are not engaged in conversation, look around the room – and when you make contact with someone, be sure to smile.

Several years ago I presented at a national engineering convention. I only went for the day, and arrived early enough to walk around the trade show floor during breakfast. I have never experienced an event like what unfurled before me:

everyone was looking at the floor as if they had lost money or an earring! They had this "death before eye contact" mentality, which made it very difficult for me to interact with them.

When in a Group, Make Eye Contact with Everyone When You Talk

Furthermore, when you are in a conversation – whether with one person or five – make sure to make eye contact with everyone, especially when you are talking. Don't just talk to the one or two people that you know.

This actually happens a lot. I've seen it in countless meetings, much less in networking forums. When someone is too focused on me, but other people are part of the conversation, I tend to find myself attempting the 'eye handoff,' trying to get the talker to look at another person.

Just make sure that you spread the eye love around when you have the floor!

Always be Polite – But Don't Answer Prying or Inappropriate Questions

Some people avoid networking events because they fear the inappropriate questions. You must always be polite, but don't feel obligated to answer someone that is getting too personal or asking prying questions.

They may ask: "Do you like your job?" Or, "Is it true that [coworker] is a real jerk?" Or perhaps, "Do they pay you well?"

Ask a business developer if their firm is busy, and they'll always say yes! They may be busy looking for work, and not necessarily busy on projects, but the business developer is telling the truth: busy! "We're always looking for the next project" is a simple, appropriate response if you get this question about workload.

Give the questioner a generic answer, and either move the conversation on to something else, turn the tables and ask the same question to them, or find an excuse to end the conversation.

REMEMBERING NAMES

We all meet many new people, and remembering their names can be a challenge. One simple technique is to use the person's name in conversation. "So Teri, how long has your company been in business?" The combination of using their name while looking at them helps to cement a visual association in your mind.

If the person has any notable or memorable features, try to connect those features with their name. You might not remember that my name is Scott, but if you silently nickname me Balding Scott or Big Forehead Scott, you have a better chance of remembering my name!

Sometimes connecting a person's name involves going beyond anything specific about them other than their name. One of my coworkers is a dynamic business developer named Kerry Wolfe. We knew each other for several years before working together, and it just so happens that my childhood dog was named Kerry. So "Kerry like my dog" became a mental association and also helped me remember how to correctly spell her name – and the dog/wolf connection was an added bonus! Another contact is named Geoff, and he mentally became "Geoff with a G."

Alliteration is good to incorporate. If you meet someone named Ben who spends a lot of time in the gym, "Biceps Benjamin" might be a good way to remember his name! Rhyming is another convention to use to help remember names.

Finally, connect on LinkedIn. Most professionals have photos, and the act of scrolling your newsfeed and seeing their posts will help cement the name with the face, so long as you pay attention to who is posting and look at their photo, not just the content they share!

Sometimes, People will have Inside Information

Occasionally people know more about you or your company than they should. I recall years ago when work was slow, someone came up to me, introduced themselves, and said "I understand your firm is on 32-hour workweeks."

That's certainly not a great conversation starter, and it actually kind of surprised me. My response was, "Wow, you have good sources. Yes, that is true – we have a great team in place and have a hopefully short valley in our workload – this way we can keep the team together and not lose any staff." Fortunately, we were soon busy and back to 40 hours. And while it used to be that having layoffs and reduced workweeks created a very negative connotation (e.g., must not be a good firm), with The Great Recession and the uneven recovery that followed, few firms avoided this unfortunate reality. But that is still nothing that I'd typically want to talk about at a networking event – whether it is my firm or someone else's firm. When a conversation begins that way, I immediately feel like I'm being put on the defensive.

When you get an inappropriate question and don't have a ready response, just say, "I'm not comfortable talking about that." Or, try a bit of humor: "How about them Patriots?" That's an easy way of letting your conversation partner know to change the subject.

Write Pertinent Information on the Back of Business Cards

When you do finally exchange business cards, turn over the other person's card and make a few notes. You can do this in front of the person, or immediately after the conversation ends.

You won't do this with every card, but sometimes there will be a piece of information that you'll really want to remember. It might be a fact about them, it might be a follow-up that you promised. If you write a note on the card, you will remember both the "who" as well as the "what." And people certainly don't mind seeing you do this – it demonstrates attentiveness to the conversation.

Don't Talk Trash

Not only are there close-talkers at networking events, there are also trash talkers. They bash their company, coworkers, former coworkers, clients, competitors, and vendors.

Do you think they have a very good reputation? Run away from these folks, and fast!

An organization I was involved with years ago had the ultimate trash talker. His venom targeted his competitors and, amazingly, even other event attendees. However, his primary trash talk concerned his company and his co-workers. He was always bashing them for everything. It was kind of a joke among other attendees … how long will it take John to bash his company today?

Twenty seconds? I bet two minutes…

Smiling is Contagious … so is a Positive Attitude

You've seen the word "smile" written several times in this book, and there is an important reason for it. If you smile, you are likeable and approachable. It shows warmth and makes others feel comfortable. People remember smilers. They like smilers. Be a smiler, and people will want to talk with you.

Get Others to Talk About Themselves or Their Companies

Much of your role as a networker is to find out about the people you meet. You want to learn about them as people, and about their companies. You want to know about their needs and what they are looking for … everyone networks for a reason. What is theirs?

Use People's First Names, Often

This is a great tip, and it applies to any conversation – as well as letters and emails. Use the other person's first name. It shows respect and interest, while also demonstrating that you view them as more than just an anonymous conversation. Using first names is a good step on the way to developing a relationship.

Don't be Obvious When Looking at Nametags

Okay, we all forget names. Sometimes it is people we met twenty years ago. Other times, it is people that we met twenty seconds ago!

Here's the deal: when you shake someone's hand, look at their nametag. Make a mental note of their name and company, and any other identifier – some nametags have titles, some include licenses or certifications – or whether they are on an organization's board, a speaker at the program, etc.

Then, don't get caught peaking again. Of course, you're going to want to refer to the nametag again. Just wait for the opportune moment. If you are engaged one-on-one in conversation, there may never be a good time. But if others are involved with the conversation, when he or she looks at one of those people, take a quick glance at their nametag again.

I've heard, "Scott, seriously? You don't remember who I am?" on more than one occasion. It's not a good feeling!

Read Body Language & Know When to Move On

Every conversation runs an arc. If you overstay your welcome, the other person's body language will provide the evidence. Pay attention to it.

Maybe they are bored. Determine if it is you or the topic of conversation. Or maybe you are talking too much and need to shut up so they can participate!

Also, by paying attention to other people's nonverbals, you will be able to see clues to determine whether to join a conversation – or not.

Be Inviting & Approachable

You do this with your body language and eye contact. You do this with smiles. You do this by where you are standing and how you are standing. The purpose of attending a networking event is to meet and talk with people. Make sure you are someone that others would want to approach and start a conversation with.

Be Authentic & Let Your Personality Shine Through

At the end of the day, people respond positively to authenticity. And they can see poseurs a mile away! Never try to be someone that you're not. The worst-case scenario is that they know you are faking it from the very first conversation. The best-case scenario is that they buy the "fake you" initially, but as they get to know you better, they uncover the truth. This behavior is off-putting. Don't make promises you can't keep. Don't try to make people think you have a role in your company that you do not. Don't take credit for something you didn't do. Don't say that you know someone that you've never really met.

However, it is difficult to fault people for doing these things. In fact, there is something known as "Imposter Syndrome," whereby talented, knowledgeable, and successful people have self-doubt. They feel like a fake, and fear other people seeing through them. How ironic is that? They've earned their success and have much to offer, yet are somewhat sheepish and feel the need to play up other strengths or connections that they don't actually have. (Or they have so much self-doubt that they are too terrified to attend networking events.)

People want to know the real you, whether it is at work, at play, or at a networking event. Everyone has something to offer, so let your real personality shine through. If you are nervous at a networking event, it's okay to share that with your conversation partner as you develop rapport: "I don't go to a lot of networking events, so this is a little intimidating for me." That's the kind of refreshing honesty that buys respect, and your conversation partner may just surprise you with a response like, "Well then I think there's three people you really need to meet tonight. Let me introduce you…"

It's okay to be reserved. It's okay to feel that you're perhaps not as accomplished as some others. Networking is actually a path to take that will help you overcome shyness and elevate your career. Just be authentic about who you are and what you do!

Look for Similarities

Whenever you are talking with someone, try to find something in common. It could be where you went to college, where you used to work or live, what sports you or your children play or enjoy, or any one of a million other things.

Always look to make a personal connection, because it is a great way to generate further conversation and make yourself more interesting and likeable. Personal connections are the foundation for relationship building.

Find out how to Help the Person You are Talking With

Everyone could use help with something. What does your conversation partner need help with? Is this something you can provide? If not, do you know someone who could help them? Remember, networking is sharing. When you determine that someone belongs in your network, you should always be looking for ways to help them – or introduce them to someone who can.

Speak Up

Are you a soft talker? Do you work with any soft talkers? You know, the ones you have to strain to listen to in a quiet room, and no one can hear on conference calls. There's no place for soft talking in a networking environment, unless you are having a private, hushed conversation. Otherwise, speak louder than you normally do; networking events can get quite noisy, and if the other person can't hear you, what's the point in having a conversation? Look for their nonverbals – are they leaning toward you or cupping their hand to their ear? If so, speak up.

Don't go for the Jugular

Networking is meeting and helping, not selling. Never try to sell. It is off-putting and people that could become a valuable part of your network will not want you to be in theirs.

Sure, talk briefly about your company and what you do. But don't corner someone and say "So do you have any work?" or "How do I get business with your firm?" That's a poor technique for salespeople, and certainly a poor technique for networkers. Let your relationship develop organically, and opportunities will follow.

Avoid Discussing the "Unholy Trinity": Politics, Religion, Money

Sometimes it seems hard to avoid politics, particularly during an election cycle. However, it is best to steer clear or move the conversation on to another subject. I was at an event with quite a few staff members of elected officials, representing several political parties. The person introducing the speaker insulted the US President from the lectern – which made for some awkward post-program networking!

Never assume that the person you are speaking with has the same political views that you do. And even if they do, they may very well not want their political leanings out there at a networking venue. If you knew that there was at least a 50% chance that the words about to come out of your mouth would make the other person uncomfortable (or even angry), would you utter them? Of course not!

Likewise, keep religion off the table. Even people who share the same faith may have vastly different beliefs. Don't assume others share your beliefs, so avoid discussing religious issues.

Finally, money is also a dangerous topic – particularly when it comes to personal finance. Don't tell your conversation partner that you just purchased a new Jaguar and then ask what they drive. It may very well put them on the defensive when they talk about their 12-year-old minivan with 180,000 miles! Incidentally, this has nothing to do with their financial situation; remember, Sam Walton, founder of Walmart, drove an old, beat-up pickup truck!

People don't care about how much money you make, how much you got paid for a recent consulting gig, or how you just joined a new country club. Don't be one of those people! It demonstrates that your value system is tied to possessions and money, not relationships and work ethic. Which type of person would you rather have in your network?

Don't Be A Complainer

Crazy as this one sounds, the reality is that there seems to be a few people at every networking event that have a "sky is falling!" attitude. They're not happy about anything. It cost too much to attend the event. The quality of the program stunk. The food selection is poor. There is only one drink ticket, not two. The venue is too far out of the way or not nice enough. The weather is crappy.

You've experienced these people, and probably looked for an exit to make your escape. Nobody wants to be around complainers, so if you find yourself being critical, pause and consider how your attitude is affecting others. You'll certainly be memorable – but not in a good way!

End Conversations Gracefully

Sometimes you'll want to move on to the next conversation, but your conversation partner has you locked in their verbal grasp! You don't want to be rude, but you'd really like to move on to interact with others. Here's a few things to say to expedite your escape:

Often, simply reaching out your hand and saying "Nice to meet you" or "Nice to talk with you" is enough to let your conversation partner know that the conversation is over. And 95% of people understand, because they do the same thing and they, too, want to talk with others. Every once in a while, however, you many have someone that stalks you through the event! So you need to be a bit more direct.

"Thank you so much for spending time chatting with me! There's a few other people I want to talk with before I leave." Reach out your hand to shake theirs, then add, "I hope to catch up with you again soon."

"Tom, I've enjoyed our conversation, but I need to duck out to use the restroom. It was a pleasure to meet you." (Make sure you actually do head to the restroom, – you don't want to make the other person feel badly.)

"I've been working my way toward the drink line, so I'm going to continue my quest! It was a pleasure meeting you."

Be polite, but don't allow yourself to be stuck with an unwanted appendage all night – particularly if you've decided that the two of you don't have much to offer one-another.

Offer to Follow-Up or Suggest Next Steps

This is more than just offering to simply pass on information. Depending upon where the conversation goes, you may want to provide some intelligence or data. Say, "I'll call you tomorrow" or "I'll send an email with the article." Offer a next step: "There seems to be a lot of commonality between us … I'd sure like to learn more about what you do. Is it okay if I call you next week to schedule a lunch meeting?"

Volunteer to Help

If you're uncomfortable at networking events, or just don't feel part of the "clique," offer to help. Perhaps you can be a greeter, or work at the registration desk. This will give you something to do, while creating the opportunity to interact with others. You'll meet a lot of fellow attendees by doing this, and it can help you ease into a networking mindset.

Join a Committee or Board

Many networking events are related to organizations run by volunteer boards and committees. A sure-fire way to fast-track your networking is to become a vital component of the organization. Consider joining the program committee or logistics committee to help plan the "what" and "where" of an event. Or join the sponsorship committee to help raise funds for the events, or marketing committee to help promote them.

Doing this will allow you to get to know a number of people involved with the organization or group, and create the foundation for a solid relationship. These fellow committee members may be connectors or influencers themselves, and can often offer introductions to other regular attendees that you'd like to meet.

Ultimately, if there is an opportunity to serve at the board level – in the case of a local chapter of a professional society, for instance – by all means, seize it! Become a leader in the organization. Doing so will make you more visible, and create greater opportunities to interact with attendees at events. There may even be a public speaking role for you along the way (don't fear it!), like thanking sponsors or introducing speakers. Standing up in front of a group enhances your credibility, and makes others feel more comfortable approaching you.

Take a Break or Grab a Seat When Your Mind is "Done"

All good things must come to an end. Often networking events are held before a meal or a program. When your mind is done, don't push it anymore. Go sit at a table or go take your seat for the program. Other people will soon join you and you'll be engaged in conversation once again. Or go home – or back to the office – if there is no program that follows.

You Don't Have to Stay Until the End

There is no rule that says that you must close an event!

Put in the effort, and don't just go for thirty minutes and leave. After you've been there for an hour or ninety minutes for a two-hour event, that may be enough.

We all have lives, we all have work, we all of stuff to do. If you force yourself to stay the entire time for every event you attend, you'll begin to resent networking events. And that helps no one. Go, have a few meaningful conversations, seek out the people you want to talk with, check off your goals, and split. That's okay. (Unless you are merely there to collect business cards!)

Questions to Ask

The easiest way to keep a conversation flowing smoothly is to ask questions of your conversation partner(s). The best questions are open-ended (and not simple yes-no questions) and allow the other people to talk about themselves, their experiences, or their companies and institutions. But don't just ask the questions – listen attentively, and their responses will drive further discussions. Here's a number of questions to have at the ready to start and drive a conversation:

- Tell me about yourself?
- What brings you here?
- What is your role at your firm/institution?
- What does your company/institution do?
- What do you do for fun?
- Where did you go to college?
- Where did you grow up?
- How'd you end up here (geographic location)?
- Do you follow sports?
- How long have you been doing (what you do)?
- What's the coolest project you've worked on?
- What's the craziest thing you've experienced in business (or on a project)?
- What does your spouse / partner / significant other do?
- What activities are your children involved with?
- What gets you out of bed in the morning?
- What's next for your career?
- What's interesting about you (or your family)?
- What makes your company different (from your competitors)?
- How is your name pronounced (or spelled)?
- Are you working on anything fun right now?
- Have any of your projects won awards?
- What's the best _____ book you've read (business, design, etc.)?
- What industry blogs or websites do you follow?
- What trends are impacting your clients right now?
- Do you volunteer for any organizations?
- Do you have any licenses or certifications?
- What's your proudest accomplishment?
- How's the economy impacting your firm?

- How many offices does your firm have?
- How many students live on your campus? (example for higher-ed contact)
- Are you funding any roadway projects in your next budget? (example for a local elected official)
- What interested you about the speaker's topic?
- What did you think about the program?
- Are you a member of this organization?
- Do you recommend that I join this organization?
- How'd you end up being a _____ (whatever they do for a living)?
- If you had it to do all over again, would you still be a _____ (whatever they do for a living)?
- What's the best part of your job?
- What don't you like about your profession?
- Have you traveled anywhere interesting recently?
- What's your next trip (or vacation)?
- What do you recommend I see or do while I'm in town (if you are traveling, and speaking with someone who lives in the area)?
- How can I help you?
- Is it okay if I reach out to you next week?

How to Determine if Someone Belongs in Your Network

What does it actually mean if someone is "in your network"? It means that you are in regular contact with one-another. It means that there is a mutually-trusting, mutually-beneficial relationship. It means that if you have the chance to help them, you will. And if they have the chance to help you, they will. So what are the criteria for elevating a contact into your network? Here's a few rules.

Can They Help Your Career?

Do they have the ability to help you or your career in some way? Perhaps they can introduce you to someone important or provide a unique source of knowledge. Maybe they can help you obtain a promotion or a new job – or even invite you to speak at a prestigious conference or blog on a well-respected website.

Can They Help Your Company?

Are they in a position to help your company? Are they decision-makers? Can they hire your firm – or put your firm in a position to win new projects or hire prospective employees? Even if they are not a decision-maker, are they an influencer – someone who's opinion matters to the ultimate decision-maker(s)? Or, can they perhaps refer your firm to a potential client?

Do They Know Someone that can Help You or Your Company?

Maybe they can't help you directly, nor help your firm directly, but they know someone who can. These are your connectors, and they are vital to having a robust network.

Will They Eventually be in a Position to Help You or Your Company?

Maybe they can't help you or your company right now, but they will be able to help you in the future. Perhaps they are up-and-comers – the cliched people "who are going places." Get them in your network now – you might be more of a resource to them in the short term, but in the long term they will be extremely valuable to you and your company.

Do You Have Something to Offer Them?

Networking is a two-way street. If you simply look at a potential network connection in terms of what they can do for you, and not what you can do for them, your relationship will not go far. Networking is giving; networking is sharing. If you don't have something to offer them directly, find someone who does. Be their connector.

Ultimately, you need round pegs in round holes … don't try to force square pegs where they don't belong. Your relationship will not be one of mutual respect and benefit, and thus not long-lasting.

Potential Stories to Bring

Because networking involves conversation, you want to make sure you are not at a lack for words when it is your turn to speak. Even though you'll be listening more than talking, the spotlight will fall on you from time-to-time. Make sure you have something to say!

You may have heard that people don't remember facts and figures, but they do remember stories. With that knowledge in hand, go into a networking event armed with several potential stories to share. Here are some ideas:

Something Interesting that Happened Recently

Think about something interesting, or humorous, that happened to you recently. Maybe on your drive to the event. Or in a meeting. Or even something that happened to someone else – so long as you're not embarrassing that person and talking negatively about them!

A Project You are Working On (Non-Confidential)

Talk about something interesting that you are working on – so long as it doesn't violate confidentiality agreements or NDA's. People will be very intrigued to learn about some of your project experiences. Depending upon the audience, a common question might be, "So what are you working on right now?" A new hospital, school, or widget manufacturing facility might be a fascinating story to tell. But so will a brownfield cleanup or replacement of a crumbling bridge. Take pride in what you do!

How You Ended up Doing What You Do

How did you end up becoming an architect, engineer, contractor, acoustician, environmental scientist, or planner? What led you down the path? Did you always want to do it, or was it a career by chance? If you had to do it all over again, would you make the same decision? One of the executives at my firm, a licensed engineer, is extremely creative and has a passion for architecture. I've heard him say several times, "Maybe I should have been an architect!"

The Best Part of Your Job

What do you like best about your job? The projects? The people? The challenges? These are some of the things that get you out of bed in the morning – the reason you do what you do.

The Worst Part of Your Job

Be very careful with this one! This is not about your company or your co-workers. However, it could be the long hours at municipal meetings. It could be that you are doing everything in BIM, but your clients aren't doing anything with the model. Within a professional association forum, you may find a bit of 'support group' happening around you: architects lament that the clients are taking four months to pay their bills; engineers lament that it takes forever to get paid by architects; marketers lament that as a non-core function in their company, their positions aren't viewed on the same level as the billable staff!

Something from a Prior Job

Maybe something really interesting happened on a previous project, or at a previous employer. Maybe you got to travel some place really cool, or visit a place that not many people can go.

Something Humorous, Particularly if it is Self-Deprecating

Humor is always great at networking events but don't tell jokes, which almost never work. Self-deprecating humor – essentially making fun of yourself – is always safe. Because my network includes quite a few public speakers, we often swap "presentation horror stories." If you present enough, you'll develop quite a backlog of stories – about the time you fell off the stage, presented with food stuck to your teeth, were interrupted by a fire alarm, or presented at a national conference with flame red eyes because the desert air caused infections in both eyes (or is that just me?)!

Places You've Recently Visited

These places could be work-related, or could be personal-related. Have you taken a cool vacation recently? Traveled somewhere exotic? Or taken your child off to their freshman year of college?

Information from an Article You Recently Read

Have you read something interesting recently? About the industry? Or the economy? Or anything else? That could be a great conversation piece. If it is related to your audience – like a trend or new technology coming down the pike – the people you are speaking with will probably have some "skin in the game," so they will appreciate what you are sharing. Offer to follow-up by sending them the article or link to your source.

Personal Connection with the Speaker

A lot of networking happens before or after programs featuring speakers or panel discussions. Do you have some connection with one of the presenters? Are they a client or a friend? Does their topic relate to something that you are working on or looking to get into?

After the Event

OK, so now the event is over. You've gone back to your office or home, had a good night's sleep, and you're back at the office. What's next?

Do not ignore the networking that you just concluded – you're not off the hook just yet, because there's still some work to be done. Here's a few tips:

Capture Information that You Don't Want to Forget

If you didn't take diligent notes on the back of business cards, you may want to capture critical information so you don't forget.

List the names of the people you spoke with, and anything you can remember about them. Note if they are a candidate for your network, or someone else's. Are they influencers or connectors? Did they share anything of note with you – a lead, a potential client, a future employee?

Get them into your CRM pronto! Your CRM could be industry-specific, like Deltek Vision or Cosential. Or it could simply be Microsoft Outlook. In fact, your CRM could be an Excel Spreadsheet, OneNote, or old-fashioned hand-written notes in folders. But whatever your CRM is, make sure you capture the information for easy future reference. Add them to your appropriate mailing lists or marketing campaigns.

The Next Day

In some cases you will want to follow-up immediately. If there is need for further introduction or action, send an email or letter. In modern-day networking, it is common to connect with someone via social media, particularly LinkedIn. By the way, if you are not on LinkedIn, get on there now! And if your background section is not completed, make sure to do so. And upload a photo. LinkedIn doesn't just help you, it helps others, too.

While emails and letters are perfectly acceptable, many people drop a connection request with a short note: "Sarah, it was great to meet you last night at the XYZ event. Here's a link to the organization I mentioned: www.smps.org. I look forward to connecting again with you soon."

As an added bonus, when you communicate through LinkedIn, it becomes your CRM.

Share Information

If you have determined that someone belongs in your network, you may want your first follow-up to be something of value for them. This could be an article related to a topic you spoke about, a potential lead for their business, information about a program they may be interested in, or an offer to introduce them to someone in your network that may be valuable for their network, too.

EXAMPLES OF GIVING

- Share an article or website with a contact
- Introduce a contact to someone that should be in their network
- Write a letter or testimonial on a contact's behalf
- Share a blog written by a contact with your LinkedIn connections
- Send a small gift and thank-you note to a contact
- Give a quality lead to a contact
- Forward an RFP to a contact whose company pursues that type of work
- Ask a contact to be part of your team for a pursuit

Conduct Research

Now you need to get to know your new contacts better. Check out their LinkedIn profile or bio on their company website, if there is one. Google them. Make notes about people in their network – do you know any of them? (LinkedIn will tell you connections in common.)

Don't immediately pounce on them and say, "Introduce me to these ten people!" But as you develop a relationship, it's okay to begin asking them about someone you want to know.

Instead of asking directly for an introduction, at least at first, say, "I see you are connected with John Doe. Do you know him well? He's someone that I think hires architects and engineers. Any advice on the best way for me to reach him?"

They might offer to introduce you. Or, they may say, "He never answers his phone, but his executive assistant is named Heather – she should be your first point of contact."

There's a tried and true way of getting to know people better, and that is the MacKay 66.

Businessman Harvey Mackay wrote a book many years ago called *Swim with the Sharks Without being Eaten Alive*. In the book, he recommends 66 data points that you should collect for clients and prospective clients: birthdays, names of spouses and children, colleges they attended, etc. Surf here to download a PDF of the Mackay 66 Customer Profile: http://www.harveymackay.com/wp-content/uploads/2016/01/mackay66.pdf .

Grow & Nurture Your Network

Growing and nurturing your network will be a challenge. If you don't make time for it, your network will wither. You will get busy with project work, management responsibilities, and any number of other things, and you will ignore your network. This is unacceptable, so make time every week to develop your network. If your only contact is a chance meeting at a networking event, then your network will never grow. You need to put effort into the relationship. A good tip is to put time on your calendar every week to focus on network nurturing.

Maintain Regular Contact

If you want your network to grow, if you want your relationships to grow, you need to cultivate and nurture them. The first way to do this is simply to be visible. Shoot your network contacts an occasional email to check in. Reach out via LinkedIn. Retweet one of their Tweets. Call them to share some news or insight. Make sure you are in regular contact with them – once a month, once every other month. If they are active on LinkedIn – and you are, too – you'll see one-another's posts. Like them, share them, comment on them.

Recognize Potential Leads

We are exposed to leads every day, but we tend to have myopia for leads that don't directly relate to us. However, most of the leads we experience are leads for others – including those in our network.

Learn to recognize these leads, then share them with the person in your network who could benefit. Just think of the vendors that call on you. You probably come across many potential leads for them – other projects you are working on, contractors or owners that may be interested in their product or service, etc. Share these opportunities with them, and they may begin sending more leads your way.

Sell Your Contacts' Services

Sometimes it makes sense to sell other people's services. When you are having a conversation with someone and recognize a lead for another member of your network, start promoting them to your conversation partner. Maybe it will work out, maybe it won't. But you'll have done them a big favor. Make sure you follow-up with your network contact to let them know that you identified an opportunity and recommended them. Provide contact information, if appropriate, so they can follow up.

Always Have a Sense of Urgency

It seems that we attach a sense of urgency to everything these days, and networking is no exception – particularly if there is a lead for a networking contact, or they have asked for information or introductions. Don't waste time – respond quickly.

Do Not Expect Instant Reciprocation

Earlier I wrote that your role in networking is Santa Clause. It is about giving, not getting.

If you share a lead, don't expect an immediate return lead. If you make an introduction, don't expect one in return (unless you ask). You may "give" three or five or even ten times before there is reciprocation. And that is okay because you are building trust and developing a relationship. And remember that "giving" could be an article, an introduction, a recommendation, or a lead.

However, there also comes a point when it becomes totally apparent that the relationship is one-sided. When this happens, it's time to move on. Take that person out of your network. Keep in mind, however, that there was a reason you put the connection in your network to begin with. So occasional contact is still appropriate – but focus on your other, higher-value networking contacts first.

Be Thankful, Appreciative & Communicative

Always be appreciative whenever someone does something for you. You do not need to reciprocate immediately, but you do need to thank them. Call them. Mail them a hand-written note. Send a gift. Let them know what you did with that "gift" they gave you – how you put the article into action, how things worked out with the conversation you had, whether or not you interviewed the employee candidate, how you followed up on the lead.

Keep Quality Data

Networks need maintenance, and you need a maintenance log of some sort. It could be hand-written notes, Outlook notes, Cosential CRM, whatever the case may be. You'll want some sort of record of your conversations, information given, information received, etc. Don't just put a new contact into your CRM; make their file or CRM record a living document that you update every time you communicate with them.

Treat Confidential Information as Such

This one seems obvious, but it is always good to ask. When someone shares information with you, ask if it is confidential. If it is, be respectful, and don't do anything that would break that confidence.

Ask Permission Before Mentioning a Contact's Name

If one of your networking contacts tells you that Acme is planning to build a new plant, and Wile E. Coyote is the person to contact, ask if it is okay to mention your networking contact's name. Sometimes they will say, "Sure, tell Wile E. that I recommended that you call him." Other times they will say, "I'd rather you didn't – I don't know him, and the information came from another source in their company." Respect the wishes of the other person.

Follow-Up with Lead Sources

Whenever a lead of any sort is given to you, move forward with it or pre-qualify the opportunity and don't. Either way, close the loop with your networking contact and let them know if you acted on it or not, what you did, and what the results were. Don't leave them in a vacuum.

Give a Gift for a Quality Lead

When someone gives you a lead that ends up resulting in a project – or it was just a really good opportunity even if you didn't get it – send a little gift of some sort.

Once a contact called me for some intelligence, and names of people that could help his prospect. I provided both. A few days later, a package showed up in the mail with a short thank-you note and a really cool pen that looked like an Exacto knife – one of the coolest pens I've seen. In this case he sent a gift before even knowing if the information I gave him was helpful or not. I'll always remember that.

Likewise, I was once at a convention where there were two good contacts in my network who had never previously met. I knew one could really help the other, so I introduced them – a design firm and a consultant. Within a short period they were working together on a project. The consultant reached out to me – not just to thank me, but to ask for my PayPal email. I gave it to her, and a few weeks later a very nice "finder's fee" showed up in my account.

I'm not recommending you pay for leads, but in this case, I learned that is part of the company's M.O. If you introduce them to someone and a contract results, you get "paid" for your recommendation. Because these were two people in my network, I would have been happy with "thank you" – but hey, you won't hear me complain!

Congratulate or Console

When you learn about an event in your networking contact's life, reach out to them. Congratulate them for a promotion or an award. Let them know that you enjoyed the blog they wrote or presentation they gave. Likewise, if you become aware of a loss in their life, send your condolences or flowers.

Offer Advice or Knowledge; Help with Brainstorming

Earlier when we reviewed how to act at a networking event, I recommended not to offer advice that is not asked for. This is absolutely true – particularly when you have just met someone. However, as you develop a trusting relationship with a good network connection, it is acceptable and appropriate to offer advice and insight.

After a conversation, you may want to send an email with a few thoughts or observations on the topic of discussion. Or if you identify a need that you can help with, say "Let's get together for coffee and brainstorm your situation" (or presentation or whatever).

Strive to be a source of knowledge for your network.

Provide Free or Discounted Services

Tread lightly with this one. There are some cases when your networking contact needs services that you or your firm provides. Maybe it makes sense for you to do a bit of free upfront work, or discount services to help them get to the next place.

Keep in mind that this service might be something the company offers – or a unique skillset that you provide. Several years ago, I developed a positive relationship with the mayor and economic development director in my community. They asked for suggestions about how to better market the city, and over a holiday break I created a marketing plan for them. They implemented some of my recommendations; others they did not, but they were very appreciative for the suggestions and ultimately asked me to be involved with other endeavors. A few years later they hired my firm for a project.

However, before you make any offer for free services, make sure you have company approval!

Get to Know Their Business, Services, Competitors…

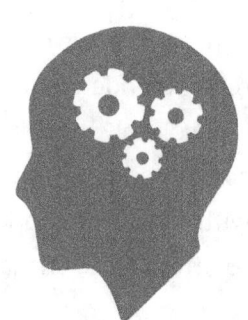

Do your networking contacts a big favor. Get to know all you can about what they do, the markets they serve, the companies they compete against, the types of needs they may have, and anything else. It will make you a more valuable network contact to them, and often the more value you can provide them, the more valuable they will be to you!

Final Thoughts

Rightsize Your Network

How big should your network be? Understand that you will meet hundreds of people in business: clients, potential clients, vendors, other A/E/C professionals, code officials, community and business leaders, and more.

But only some of them belong in your true "network."

There are many different recommendations out there, but the 100-150-person range seems to be a doable number. This means 100-150 relationships that you must nurture.

Just because you have 300 or 500 or 1000 LinkedIn contacts doesn't mean that they all need nurtured. In fact, there are probably a lot of people in your network that aren't even active LinkedIn users – or you can't remember how or why you originally connected with many of them!

Track Your Network

Track your network, track your network, and track your network!

I can't emphasize this enough, which is why you're reading about it again. Be diligent about tracking all the activities that you do with every person. Find out what they are doing and make note of it.

If you haven't communicated with someone in a year, they aren't really in your network, are they? This doesn't mean that you need weekly or even monthly contact with everyone in your network, but by tracking you'll be able to determine where you need to put some effort to make sure that your networking contacts don't grow cold.

Prune Your Network Annually or Seasonally

This is important. People who once made sense to be in your network may no longer fit the bill. Prune them. Maybe they can't help you or your company – or can't influence or connect – and won't be able to do so in the future.

It's not like you are going to call them and say, "Steve, you are no longer in my network. Have a great life."

Your network needs to be dynamic. Just as you'll regularly be adding people, you'll also regularly be removing people. That's the nature of maintaining a network.

If you aren't showing value to others (read: giving), you will get pruned from their network.

How Can I Help You?

So that brings up my final question. How can I help you? You just finished reading this book. Do you think I belong in your network? Is there some way I can help you? How will you reciprocate?

Here's a few thoughts:

Should we brainstorm where you should be networking?

Could we develop a strategy for raising your visibility?

Can we talk about your next networking event and discuss your stories to tell or questions to ask?

Can I coach you in networking and take you to an event?

These are questions I typically ask at the end of my networking presentation, when I'm physically in front of an audience; however, these questions are less relevant for a book. And yet, it's always worthwhile determining if someone belongs in your network!

Cheat Sheet

Why Networking is Important

- Find Project Opportunities
- Meet Decision Makers
- Meet "Connectors" & "Influencers"
- Meet Peers & Competitors
- Learn Trends
- Gain Competitive Intelligence
- Identify Potential Hires
- Career Fallback

What Networking Is & Isn't

- Networking is Connecting, Not Collecting
- Networking is Foundation Building
- Networking is Building Trust
- Networking is Giving
- Networking is Not Schmoozing
- Networking is Not "Drinks with Friends"
- Networking is Not Instant Business
- Quality is Far Superior to Quantity
- Networking is for Everyone
- Extroverts Like to Talk
- Introverts Would Rather Ask Questions Than Talk About Themselves
- Ambiverts are Able to Balance Extrovert & Introvert Behaviors

Who Belongs in Your Network?

- Clients
- Former Clients
- Potential Clients
- Vendors
- Co-Workers (Including at Other Offices)
- Former Co-Workers
- Community & Business Leaders
- Professional Association Contacts
- College Alumni
- Personal Friends
- Family Members
- Former Network Members
- Parents of Children's Friends – or Friends of Children

Before the Event

- Know Why You Are Going (Or Not Going)
- Organize Your Business Cards
- Know How to Wear Your Nametag
- Know How to Shake Hands
- Wear Proper Attire
- Know Your Audience
- Find Out Who Will be Attending
- Come Equipped with Questions to Ask
- Come Equipped with Stories to Share
- Prepare Three "Speeches"
  - About You
  - About Your Role
  - About Your Company
- Use the "Best/Test"

Know Thyself

- What do You Do?
- What are Your Hobbies?
- What is Your Education & Experience?
- What are Your Proudest Accomplishments?
- What Does Your Spouse / Partner / Significant Other Do?
- What Activities are Your Children Involved With?
- What are You Passionate About?
- What are Your Goals – or What is on Your Bucket List?
- Where are you From?
- What is Interesting About You or Your Family?
- What Differentiates Your Firm from the Competitors?

During the Event

- Put Your Day Neatly Away in a Box
- Get Energized
- Brush Your Breath
- Arrive Early
- Check the Nametag Table to See Who has Yet to Arrive
- Don't Stress – Take a Few Breaths
- Remember the Platinum Rule

- Qualify the Person
- Hang Out by the: Entrance, Bar, or Food
- Get in a Line
- Minimize Eating & Drinking
- Find a Standing-Only Table
- Scan the Room
- Seek Out Clients & Potential Clients
- Find the Lone Wolf
- Know How to Join a Conversation
- Lurk & Listen
- Tap Someone You Know
- Walk Up, Smile & Extend Your Hand
- Understand Open & Closed Conversations
- Find a Wingman
- Don't Only Talk with People You Know
- Be a Listener
- Never Interrupt
- Be Conservative with Business Cards
- Take a Time Out
- Don't Hide in a Corner, Playing on Your Smartphone to Look "Busy"
- Share Liberally
- Buy a Quality Contact a Drink
- Invite People into Conversations
- Note Interesting Things that People are Wearing
- Compliment & Thank Others – But Don't Go Overboard
- Ask About Accomplishments
- Don't Ask for Free Advice – or Give Advice Unless Asked for It
- Offer to Pass Along Information
- Listen with Your Mind
- Don't Look Around the Room for Someone Else to Speak With
- Don't be a Close Talker
- Take Another Break
- Make Eye Contact with Everyone
- When in a Group, Make Eye Contact with Everyone When You Talk
- Always be Polite – But Don't Answer Prying or Inappropriate Questions
- Sometimes, People will have Inside Information
- Write Pertinent Information on the Back of Business Cards
- Don't Talk Trash
- Smiling is Contagious … so is a Positive Attitude
- Get Others to Talk About Themselves or Their Companies

- Use People's First Names, Often
- Don't be Obvious When Looking at Nametags
- Read Body Language & Know When to Move On
- Be Inviting & Approachable
- Be Authentic & Let Your Personality Shine Through
- Look for Similarities
- Find out how to Help the Person You are Talking With
- Speak Up
- Don't go for the Jugular
- Avoid Discussing the "Unholy Trinity": Politics, Religion, Money
- Don't be a Complainer
- End Conversations Gracefully
- Offer to Follow-Up or Suggest Next Steps
- Volunteer to Help
- Join a Committee or Board
- Take a Break or Grab a Seat When Your Mind is "Done"
- Don't Feel that You Have to Stay Until the End

How to Determine if Someone Belongs in Your Network

- Can They Help Your Career?
- Can They Help Your Company?
- Do They Know Someone that can Help You or Your Company?
- Will They Eventually be in a Position to Help You or Your Company?
- Do You Have Something to Offer Them?

Potential Stories to Bring

- Something Interesting that Happened Recently
- A Project You're are Working On (Non-Confidential)
- How You Ended Up Doing What You Do
- The Best Part of Your Job
- The Worst Part of Your Profession
- Something from a Prior Job
- Something Humorous, Particularly if it is Self-Deprecating
- Places You've Recently Visited
- Information from an Article You Recently Read
- Personal Connection with the Speaker

After the Event

- Capture Information that You Don't Want to Forget
- Take Action the Next Day
- Share Information
- Conduct Research

Grow & Nurture Your Network

- Maintain Regular Contact
- Recognize Potential Leads
- Sell Your Contact's Services
- Always Have a Sense of Urgency
- Do Not Expect Instant Reciprocation
- Be Thankful, Appreciative & Communicative
- Keep Quality Data
- Treat Confidential Information as Such
- Ask Permission Before Mentioning a Contact's Name
- Follow-Up with Lead Sources
- Give a Gift for a Quality Lead
- Congratulate or Console
- Offer Advice or Knowledge; Help with Brainstorming
- Provide Free or Discounted Services
- Get to Know Their Business, Services, Competitors…

Final Thoughts

- Rightsize Your Network
- Track Your Network
- Prune Your Network Annually or Seasonally

Resources

Organizations & Societies

From *Reputation Design+Build: Creating Winning Personal Brands for Engineering, Design & Construction Professionals* by Scott D. Butcher, FSMPS, CPSM.

AACE International - http://www.aacei.org/

Academy of Geo-Professionals - http://www.geoprofessionals.org/

American Academy of Environmental Engineers and Scientists - http://www.aaees.org/

American Association of Museums - http://www.aam-us.org/

American Board of Industrial Hygiene - http://www.abih.org/

American Concrete Institute - http://www.concrete.org/

American Consulting Engineers Council - http://www.acec.org/

American Institute of Architects - http://www.aia.org/

American Institute of Constructors - http://www.professionalconstructor.org/

American Jails Association - http://www.aja.org/

American Planning Association - http://www.planning.org/

American Public Works Association - http://www.apwa.net/

American Resort Development Association - http://www.arda.org/

American Road & Transportation Builders Association - http://www.artba.org/

American Society for Healthcare Engineering - http://www.ashe.org/

American Society of Civil Engineers - http://www.asce.org/

American Society of Highway Engineers - http://www.highwayengineers.org/

American Society of Interior Designers - http://www.asid.org/

American Society of Landscape Architects - http://www.asla.org/

American Society of Professional Estimators - http://www.aspenational.org/

American Subcontractors Association - https://www.asaonline.com

Assisted Living Federation of America - http://www.alfa.org/

Associated Builders & Contractors - http://www.abc.org/

Associated General Contractors of America - http://www.agc.org/

Associated Specialty Contractors - http://www.assoc-spec-con.org/

Association for Facilities Engineering - http://www.afe.org/

Association for Preservation Technology - http://www.apti.org/

Association of Heating, Refrigerating, and Air Conditioning Engineers - http://www.ashrae.org/

Association of Physical Plant Administrators - http://www.appa.org/
BICSI - https://www.bicsi.org/

Building Owners and Managers Association International - http://www.boma.org/

Construction Financial Management Association - http://www.cfma.org/

Construction Management Association of America - http://cmaanet.org/

Construction Owners Association of America - http://www.coaa.org/

Construction Specifications Institute - http://www.csinet.org/

Construction Writers Association - http://www.constructionwriters.org/

Council of Educational Facilities Planners International - http://www.cefpi.org/

Design-Build Institute of America - http://www.dbia.org/

Illuminating Engineering Society - http://ies.org/

Institute of Electrical and Electronics Engineers - http://www.ieee.org/

Institute of Hazardous Materials Management - http://www.ihmm.org/

Institute of Real Estate Management - http://www.irem.org/

International Cost Engineering Council - http://www.icoste.org/

International Facilities Management Association - http://www.ifma.org/

International Interior Design Association - http://www.iida.org/

NAIOP Commercial Real Estate Development Association - http://www.naiop.org/

National Association of Home Builders - http://www.nahb.com/

National Association of Women in Construction - http://www.nawic.org

National Contract Management Association - http://www.ncmahq.org/

National Council for Interior Design Qualification - http://www.ncidq.org/

National Council of Architectural Registration Boards - http://www.ncarb.org/

National Council of Structural Engineers Associations - http://www.ncsea.com/

National Insulation Association - http://www.insulation.org/

National League of Cities - http://www.nlc.org/

National Registry of Environmental Professionals - http://www.nrep.org/

National Society of Professional Engineers - http://www.nspe.org/index.html

National Trust for Historic Preservation - http://www.preservationnation.org/

Precast Prestressed Concrete Institute - http://www.pci.org/

Professional Construction Estimators Association of America - http://www.pcea.org/

Project Management Institute - http://www.pmi.org/

Retail Contractors Association - http://www.retailcontractors.org/

Society for College and University Planning - http://www.scup.org/page/index

Society for Marketing Professional Services - http://www.smps.org

Society of American Military Engineers - http://www.same.org/

Society of Architectural Historians - http://www.sah.org/

Society of Cost Estimating & Analysis - http://www.sceaonline.org/

Urban Land Institute - http://www.uli.org/

US Green Building Council - http://www.usgbc.org/

Service Groups

Rotary International - www.rotary.org

Sertoma - http://www.sertoma.org/

Lions Club - www.lionsclub.org

Kiwanis International - www.kiwanis.org

Resources – Books

Emotional Intelligence 2.0 by Travis Bradberry, Jean Greaves

How to Win Friends & Influence People by Dale Carnegie

Make Your Contacts Count: Networking Know-How for Business and Career Success by Anne Baber and Lynne Waymon

Markendium by the Society for Marketing Professional Services

Network Like an Introvert: A New Way of Thinking About Business Relationships by Tim Klabunde

Networking for People Who Hate Networking: A Field Guide for Introverts, the Overwhelmed, and the Underconnected by Devora Zack

Networking is a Contact Sport by Joe Sweeney

Networking Like a Pro: Turning Contacts Into Connections by Ivan Misner, Ph.D.

Never Eat Alone by Keith Ferrazzi

The Referral Engine by John Jantsch

The 7 Habits of Highly Effective People by Stephen Covey

Swim with the Sharks Without Being Eaten Alive by Harvey Mackay

jdbIQity Services

Marketing
- Marketing Planning & Strategy
- Writing / Ghostwriting
- Collateral Material Ideation
- Digital Marketing
- Proposal Development
- Staffing Audit
- Collateral Audit
- Brand Development & Strategy
- Value Message Development
- Communications Strategy

Business Development
- Sales Planning & Strategy
- Pursuit Strategy
- Presentation Development & Support
- Capture Plans
- Staffing Audit
- Client Satisfaction & Perception Surveys / Interviews

Research
- Target Clients
- Environmental Scanning
- Competitive Analysis
- New Market Analysis

Facilitation
- Strategic Planning
- Sales Planning
- Specific Project Pursuit
- SWOT Analysis

Training & Coaching
- Business Development
- Seller-Doer
- Presentation Skills
- Writing / Content Marketing
- Networking
- Trends
- Personal Branding
- Soft Skills

Thought Leadership
- Blogging
- Books / E-books
- Presentations

Management
- Sales/Marketing Organization & Structure
- Metrics / KPIs

Interested in learning more about jdb**IQ**ity's full slate of marketing, consulting, training, and facilitation services? Contact Scott D. Butcher, FSMPS, CPSM at 717-434-1543 or sbutcher@jdbe.com.

www.jdbengineering.com/jdbiqity

About the Author

Scott D. Butcher, FSMPS, CPSM has more than 25 years of experience in the A/E/C industry. He is vice president and chief marketing officer for JDB Engineering, Inc. and two affiliate companies and also is principal and champion for jdbIQity. Scott has served on the board of directors for the Society for Marketing Professional Services and is a past president and former trustee of the SMPS Foundation.

A regular speaker at industry events, he has given more than 250 presentations to local, regional, and national events of SMPS, AIA, ACEC, AGC, PSMJ, SDA, ASCE, IFMA, USGBC, and others. A widely-published author who has written 20 books and ebooks, Scott writes Marketropolis, the sales and marketing blog on the ENR.com. His articles have been featured in *Professional Services Management Journal, Project Management, A/E Marketing Journal, The Zweig Letter, Revolutionary Marketing, Construction Executive Online, Marketer,* and *The Military Engineer,* among others. He co-authored the SMPS Foundation book, *A/E/C Business Development – The Decade Ahead,* and wrote the recent SMPS publication *Sell. Do. Win Business. How A/E/C Firms are Using Staff to Win More Work.*

Scott's books include *Reputation Design+Build: Creating Winning Personal Brands for Engineering, Design, and Construction Professionals; Simplified Project Photography: A Guide for DIY Architectural Photographers; Historic Architecture of Pennsylvania;* and *Marketing in the Building Industry,* among others. He is a Certified Professional Services Marketer and a Fellow of the Society for Marketing Professional Services.

Connect with Scott

LinkedIn: www.linkedin.com/in/scottdbutcher
Twitter: www.twitter.com/scottdbutcher

Follow Scott's Blogs

ENR Marketropolis: www.enr.com/blogs/22-marketropolis
jdbIQity: www.jdbengineering.com/blog

www.ingramcontent.com/pod-product-compliance
Lightning Source LLC
Chambersburg PA
CBHW051319220526
45468CB00004B/1407